THE CONQUEST OF FEAR

By showing how to understand the psychological reasons for irrational fear this book points the way to peace of mind for anyone who suffers from phobias, anxiety and obsessions.

THE CONQUEST OF FEAR

by

W.J. McBRIDE

A. THOMAS AND COMPANY
Wellingborough, Northamptonshire

First published by The Psychologist Magazine Ltd. 1973
This Edition 1977
Second Impression 1980

ISBN 0 85454 036 9

Printed and bound in Great Britain
by Hunt Barnard Printing Ltd., Aylesbury, Bucks.

Contents

Foreword

FEAR is commonly regarded with scorn, and fearlessness extolled as a desirable attribute. In fact, if man was without a sense of fear his survival would be severely jeopardized, since he would not have that vital mechanism which warned him of danger and motivated him in taking the necessary evasive action. Naturally, panic and hysteria are obstructive, but the ability to perceive danger is essential.

This book does not concern itself so much with this natural or rational fear, but with the psychological problems brought about by unnatural, irrational fear. It has been estimated that around one person in ten suffers from some sort of morbid fear, and is incapacitated by neuroses resulting in anxiety and compulsion.

The author traces the origins of these neurotic fears, explains their development and gives guidelines for their alleviation and eventual control. The close link between irrational fear and inferiority is discussed, and self-treatment outlined. Phobias are explained, the anxieties which result from the pressure of modern living are looked at, and the value of a true religion in combating the fear that threatens the human spirit are propounded.

For anyone who suffers from neurotic fears this book offers hope in that it will help the reader to understand more clearly the psychological background to his difficulties, and to find the way to peace.

Preface

ONE of the benefits arising from the investigations and discoveries of psychology is the clear light it has thrown on the meaning and significance of fear. At one time it was the accepted opinion that fear was the one great enemy of man.

Even to-day this belief is sometimes held by people of culture and education. A well-known author once wrote: 'Fear is the most to be loathed, the most degrading of all the emotions of the human mind. It is the enemy of progress, not only of the spirituality of the individual, but of the race.'

It is not too much to say that this judgment is not well-informed, and at best is only a half-truth.

Misunderstanding has arisen with regard to the significance of fear because the distinction is not made between fear that is natural and rational and fear that is unnatural and irrational.

Rational fear has its source in objective

reality. That is to say it is caused through some person or circumstance in the environment creating a situation of danger. The individual perceives that his existence is threatened by certain external forces or things, and he reacts to the situation with a fear emotion.

But natural fear — unless under exceptional circumstances, such as panic arising from an abnormal environmental situation — does not destroy nor paralyze the individual. This situation, in fact, would only arise if the individual in a threatening situation did *not* have any sense of fear. The creature of the species that does not perceive a dangerous situation and respond to it with caution and discretion will by its very insensitiveness destroy itself.

The perception of danger, and an adequate fear reaction, will heighten all the powers of the body (and mind) so that an escape is made possible.

The adaptation of the lower forms of life to their environment has for its meaning the preservation of the species. Modern civilization — international and social law, together with the composition and creativeness of society — has the same law as its inspiring motive.

Hence rational fear instead of being the enemy of the race is really an ally. It could even be described as a higher form of instinctive wisdom.

The fear that destroys is the unnatural fear that has no objective reality. We know, for instance, that there are very many people who are dominated by irrational fear that their friends call 'silly,' and of which they themselves are half-ashamed.

There is no threatening situation in their environment which should make them afraid yet they cannot escape from fears and negative feelings which make their lives one long-drawn-out fight against invisible foes and spectres.

It is these subjective, private, incomprehensible fears which destroy the individual. In some cases they rob the victim of all peace of mind, create disharmony within the personality and drain the nervous system of its reserve. Not infrequently they drive the sufferer to suicide and insanity as an escape.

Freud calls this form of fear *anxiety*: An abnormal negative feeling tone of the whole personality which expresses itself in various neurotic forms, and has definitive characteristics for each form.

While dealing in this book with fear in general, I shall endeavour to throw some light on the causes and characteristics of this particular condition.

W.J. McBride

1.

Fear and the Child

IN the understanding and treatment of fear it is necessary to begin at the beginning. There are exceptions, but the origin of most neurotic fears can be traced to childhood.

The seeds of fear then sown may lie dormant in the unconscious mind for many years, but sooner or later, during some period of crisis or stress, the tare seed sown in the springtime of the mind will grow up and choke the wheat of good sense. This truth is not usually recognized when adolescent or adult eccentricities are being considered for treatment.

The child is born into a world where, by the very nature of birth and development, it must submit to others' management. For a much longer time than any other young creature it is the passive recipient of impressions and experiences over which it has no control.

When ultimately it does arrive at the point where it can exercise its own powers of selection, discretion and self-determination, the foundations of its future mental and psychical house have been laid.

If the foundations have been built upon rock — upon self-reliance, courage, love and wisdom — the mental and psychical house will grow up in strength and beauty and be able to withstand the assaults of circumstance and the challenge of the world.

If it has been built upon sand — upon dependence, fear, unwise love and lack of initiative — then when the winds come and the rains descend the house will fall.

Determinative for good or ill are the impressions received from the environment during the early years of childhood. It is then that the future life-pattern is being built, for the child at that period is open to receive uncritically and almost unconsciously the impressions that stream in from the community upon its plastic mind.

Of all the influences which form the most lasting impression the major is fear. Psychologists say that at birth the child has only two fears: The fear of loud noises and the fear of falling.

This is quite natural since the new-born child is a creature of sense, and by the process of birth is launched into an entirely new world. It follows that the fear of loud noises and the fear of falling — as contrasted with the sense of pre-natal silence and security — will induce a feeling of insecurity to which the child must become accustomed.

As the awareness of life develops, however, other instinctive fears make their appearance. Remove from the environment the threatening danger of which the child is aware, give it a sense of security and protection and the fear attendant upon the particular object will vanish.

If, however, the threatening object becomes a very *real* reality, and the child suffers a physical hurt or mental shock, a fear complex may be established in the unconscious mind. This historic eventuality must always be envisaged when a child, or adult, suffers from a fear for which there is no apparent cause in immediate circumstance or contemporary history. In a later chapter I shall give one or two illustrations of this truth.

Of all the fears in childhood the major is the fear of the dark. There are several reasons for this. It is now well established that we each carry within our unconscious minds memories that run back into the primordial past of the race.

These memories find expression through our habits and instincts. They might be described as the unconscious collective wisdom of the race, as it is these hidden powers which help man to adapt himself to his environment and to preserve his existence.

In primitive ages the dark was man's greatest enemy. In the dark lurked wild things, strange peoples, unknown powers, against which man had no certain protection.

For ages when knowledge (a mere awareness

of life) burned dimly, when swiftness of foot and strength of arm were the only defences, primitive peoples were haunted by fear of the dark and what it held. This racial fear memory still persists in the unconscious mind, and is one of the factors behind the fear of the dark in children.

While it is undoubtedly true that racial fear memories influence present habits, it is also much more true that immediate environment and experience play a determinative part. A child left alone in the dark is separated from the one who gives a sense of security and courage – his mother. If a child has been unwisely trained to depend too greatly upon his parents, he will only feel secure when they are within sight or near at hand.

A sensitive child in the dark is confronted with a menacing situation that makes an assault upon his none too great powers of self-reliance and independence. He has to battle with foes and enemies in his imagination, just as primitive man had to battle with real foes and enemies which haunted the dark of his environment.

If it be said it is only imagination, it must be remembered that to a child imagination is a very real thing. A factor which has the power to bring about nervous shock should not be lightly dismissed as 'only imagination.'

Sufficient recognition has not been given to the penetrating influence of unconscious acts and thoughts of adults upon the plastic child mind. Education and child training have been too severely and unimaginatively limited to the spoken word or commandment.

Until relatively recently, both in home and school, child training was supported and enforced by an overbearing authority which had as its symbol a rod, together with the possibility of personal and social indignity for the scholar. To spare the rod was to spoil the child.

Not a few children who have been trained or subjected to the torture of this primitive cruelty have been stunted in personality development and made the enemies both of the social order and everything that stands in the name of education.

UNCONSCIOUS EDUCATION

The greater part of a child's best education is unconscious. It is won or acquired from the feeling tone and outlook of his early environment. It is this almost unconscious influence which shapes the mind and character of the child for good or ill.

The tone and quality of a home or school is more important than social status or tradition, for the child absorbs its mental and spiritual environment as a sponge does water.

This is equally true with regard to the fear actions and thoughts which dominate his environment. It is exceedingly difficult for a child to grow up mentally and psychically healthy in a neurotic atmosphere.

Panic fear is contagious; no less so is neurotic

fear. As food to the body, education to the mind, so are the healthy or unhealthy outlook and habits of its parents and teachers to a child.

One illustration of this truth will suffice. A child eight years old was terrified when travelling in a train on entering a tunnel. Her mother explained (incorrectly) that the child's fear was hereditary, as she herself, until recently, had suffered from a similar fear.

Pressed for an explanation of when and how this fear began, she said it was in her seventeenth year after an incident which need not be described. The child had frequently travelled with the mother in trains, and unconsciously had acquired a fear of tunnels, no doubt from the panic condition of the mother on such occasions.

It is to unconscious influence that most, if not all, of the irrational fears of childhood (such as fear of ghosts, strangers, animals, insects) may be traced.

There is no evidence that any (functional) psychological condition can be transmitted from parent to child. There is overwhelming evidence, however, that parental fears by unconscious suggestion, imitation and influence can be transmitted to children so that the background of their minds (the unconscious) becomes 'conditioned' to fear.

Wrong training or a hurtful (shock) experience or both constitute the main causes of irrational fears in childhood and in adult life.

AIDS TO UNDERSTANDING

As an aid to the understanding, alleviation and treatment of these fears, the following suggestions will prove helpful:

1. No child should be trained or educated by fear. Thousands of children have been maimed in mind and spirit by cruelty, violence, and incapacity, disguised in the sheep's clothing of child welfare, training and education.

Faults and wrong habits should not be treated as errors or sins, but rather as the almost necessary imperfection of the learner in the greatest of all professions — that of self-sculpture. Love, understanding, encouragement and patience should give to the child a sense of security, physical, personal and environmental.

2. A child should be guarded from all parental fears that would unconsciously make an impression upon the receptive young mind. Parents should not parade their own neurotic fears before their children.

The home life should be marked by a quiet atmosphere of confidence, understanding and sanity in the presence of anything that perplexes and disturbs. The fear of simple harmless things, such as cats, mice, etc., should be looked upon as unwomanly and childish — as they are.

In the same way, the fear of pain, the dark, and too great an anxiety about health should be looked upon as unmanly and immature.

3. To laugh at a child's fears is criminal. Imaginative fear is as real to a child as the presence of an armed bandit is to an adult. To hold fear up to ridicule — a fear that the child cannot understand and would be rid of if he could — is to create a deep sense of helplessness and insecurity in the child's mind.

No child should be allowed to fight out its own subjective fear battle without weapon, understanding or companionship.

If a child has been 'conditioned' to fear a particular thing or situation, understanding should be employed to recondition the mind so that a courageous attitude supplants the fearful.

Children who fear the dark, particularly at bed-time, should be given a night-light and a sense of being protected. When years of discretion are reached the nature and necessity of darkness should be explained.

Many a child who has been forced to sleep in a dark room, who has gone to sleep crying with terror, probably after a stormy scene and punishment, has had implanted in its mind a fear wound or complex from which it has never completely escaped. With understanding and imagination, irrational fears in children can be transformed into trust and forgetfulness.

There is a story of a child who used to suffer wracking nightmares of a big fierce tiger that came toward him in his sleep. A wise physician took him in his arms and talked to him about his imaginary visitor. He told him that the tiger was really a friendly tiger, and that the next time he saw him he was to speak to him as he would to a friendly dog.

That night the parents and the physician watched the boy after he had fallen asleep. They saw his little body grow tense for a moment, and then a hand go out as if it were patting something. Then the boy spoke: 'Hello, old fellow,' he said. At that he relaxed and fell into a refreshing sleep.

We react to life how we think and feel. If we think in the terms of fear we shall have fear feelings and act accordingly. If we think in the terms of courage, trust and confidence, we shall feel and act accordingly. As is well known, the world takes on the colour of our persistent thoughts.

2.
Fear and Inferiority

FEAR and inferiority feeling are practically synonymous terms. There would be no inferiority feeling without fear, and no fear without a sense of inferiority.

These two emotions act and react upon one another. When inferiority is felt in the presence of anyone (and inferiority is necessarily personal and social — that is to say it denotes comparisons or 'ideas of reference' between individuals) we are also afraid.

We may be afraid of others' opinion of us, afraid that their beauty or talent puts us in the shade, afraid of our own incapacity or position. This fear on its social side constitutes the essence of inferiority.

For the sake of clarity and convenience we can say that inferiority feeling is aroused by childhood experiences which we may group as follows: Wrong training, inexperience and a deep sense of psychical frustration or unfitness.

In the opinion of Dr. Adler, three types are particularly prone to develop inferiority feeling: The spoilt or pampered child; the hated or unwanted child; and the child conscious of some peculiar physical deformity or deficiency.

THE SPOILT CHILD

A spoilt child is a child who, by an unwise training, has become unfitted to be a normally social individual, a piece of machinery which has been mishandled by an unskilled craftsman so that it cannot without defect take its part in the combined working utility of the machine.

This defect is characteristic of the spoilt child. Apart from the group he may appear quite normal (in the eyes of his parents he may be the very paragon of perfection), but by the conditions of his training he cannot fit in satisfactorily as a working unit of the community.

The reason for this failure of adjustment to the group by the spoilt child is that his training has not been normal and socialized. The spoilt and pampered child is protected, cared for, isolated and removed from the stern struggle of life. The unwise love that has been showered upon him gives to the child an abnormal sense of his own importance and superiority.

In later life, under propitious circumstances, this importance and superiority takes on the form of class snobbery. By protection from the real world and its struggle, the spoilt child is unfitted to appreciate the competition of the greater world without.

If the spoilt and pampered child is fortunate enough to be able to indulge his whims and wishes and has no need to enter the competitive struggle for daily bread, he is saved from a rude awakening.

If he can keep to his 'hothouse' condition and is protected from any chill wind or circumstance, all may be well. If, however, through necessity or mishap he is forced out into the world to make his own way, win his own bread, and fight his own battles, he not infrequently develops a neurosis.

The spoilt child sent out into the world cannot understand why people should not shower on him the same love as he got from his parents. He cannot adjust himself to authority or a subordinate position. He will criticize those in authority to show how superior he is, or else he will pick a row with his boss and 'get the sack.'

Before long he will get another job and do the same again. He will move from job to job, restless and dissatisfied, simply because he cannot adjust himself to society. He lives in a mature community with the outlook and feelings of a child.

When at last he discovers that he cannot coerce the environment to his will or get society to pander — as his mother did — to his childish demands and peculiar qualities, he becomes profoundly discouraged, and escapes from the harsh brutality of the world by one of the easy doors of alcoholism, parasitism, confidence trickery, gambling, or isolation.

The flotsam and jetsam of our cities and prisons are largely drawn from the spoilt and pampered children who found that the world of men without good reason would not surrender to their emotional appeals for favouritism, consideration, and special privileges.

The spoilt children who through good fortune and circumstances have been able to rise above this challenge go to the other extreme by continually calling attention to their funny egotism.

To feed their vanity they cultivate eccentricities, perform spectacular stunts, make dramatic public exhibitions of themselves, wear conspicuous clothes, and jockey to get themselves appointed to prominent position or office.

Behind all this exhibitionism and striving for significance there lies a deep sense of inferiority due to fear. In the first group there is a profound fear of life itself. No one could slip down to these inferior attitudes and indulgences who inwardly feels competent to meet life.

The second group, fearing that their childish self-importance is not receiving the attention it should, engage in all manner of social misbehaviour and silliness to win the attention and applause of society. When they were children they won their attention by unruliness, sulking, pranks and mischief.

The spoilt child must be first, must be the

centre of attention, cannot allow a rival, must have the best seat and the right clothes, and demands unfailing deference and consideration. On the roads, in theatres, meeting-places, offices, clubs, etc., the spoilt children of civilization proclaim their emotional infantilism. By their childish bad manners they create part of the social problem of law and order.

The spoilt child of the female sex fears marriage, and will not marry because no man is good enough, or because she fears the duties and responsibilities of marriage. Should she marry, before long, unless there is a psychical change, the marriage will break down. The married overgrown child goes home to his or her mother. Both are psychically immature and fear the discipline, duties and demands of adult life.

The sentimental mother who dresses her boy up like a little girl, sows the seeds of inferiority and abnormality in the child's mind.

THE UNWANTED CHILD

The hated and unwanted child, for whatever reason, arrives by another route at the same destination. The child nutured in hate is unfitted for life, simply because all expressions of hate are anti-social. To be either hated or unwanted means that society is either against you or has no place for you.

Where punishment, criticism and repression are the persistent factors in child training, all children so treated are psychically maimed.

Discouragement, negative feeling, fear and inferiority, become the dominant dispositions of the mind.

When to. the corporal punishment of the home or environment there is added an unfavourable school environment, the consequences are often devastating. It is this fact which Dr. H. Crichton Miller had in mind when he said:

'It is sometimes supposed that great injury is done to the emotional development of pupils by corporal punishment, but I would say, from my experience, much more harm is done by the sarcastic or sneering schoolmaster than by the cane.'

When negative training is persistent the child carries the thought, memory and feeling of it into later life, and establishes a background of timidity, inferiority and fear.

The child suffering from some peculiar physical defect or deficiency, unless very wisely guided and nurtured, arrives also at manhood with a discouraged or inferior attitude to life.

To influences such as these might be traced the factors that operate to bring success to one and failure to another. It is a matter of everyday observation that two men may start out on an equal task. One makes a success and the other a failure of the venture. We are speaking now of tasks that encompass social relationship. To all intents and purposes both started on the same footing.

We take the case of two travellers: Both have

had the same training, command the same backing, carry the same commodity and are presented with the same opportunity. One sets out with self-confidence, takes everything in his stride and wins success and promotion.

The other attacks his work in the spirit of timidity, hesitation and lack of self-reliance. He cannot make contact with his customers, and fails to convince or interest them in the qualities of his commodity. He has the will and desire to succeed, knows that success or failure depend upon his efforts, yet he fails in spite of his best endeavours.

The solution to this and all similar problems of success and failure — eliminating lack of character and incapacity — lies in the mental background from which they were working. The successful traveller had a successful unconscious as well as a conscious desire to be successful. His positive emotions, built into his mind by wise training in childhood, gave him the necessary courage and power to make his contacts convincing.

The unsuccessful traveller was working from the standpoint of an unsuccessful unconscious. Strive as he would, the negative emotions or fear complexes, built into his mind by a wrong childhood training, overcame, as they always do overcome, the will of the conscious mind to be successful.

The unsuccessful traveller was beaten by his background, by his negative emotions arising from buried fear complexes. The successful traveller was helped on because there had been built into his unconscious mind a positive and wholesome attitude to reality.

It is generally useless to tell someone dominated by buried fear complexes to use will power and follow certain mental rules in order to be successful. The prime need is to have the buried complexes released. When this is done, success rules may be followed to advantage. Where success rules are in continual conflict with buried complexes the result is strain, tension, fatigue and depression.

THE POWER OF IMAGINATION

Though wrong training in childhood has a tremendous influence in the formation of an inferiority attitude, we must not forget the power of imagination. A child may be very wisely trained and may work normally from a positive approach to experience, but not infrequently in later life when confronted with a new experience upon which very much depends, imagination may play havoc with self-confidence.

The actor on a first night, because he knows he is faced with a battery of critics who will tell the merits or demerits of the play, may be naturally strained and diffident. The singer, making a first appearance, may be overcome by the occasion and fail to do justice to her talent.

The speaker confronted with an audience who will assess his thought and manner may become over-strained with emotion and fail in his task.

Imagination fills the situation with dread. Too much significance has been attached to the occasion. Self-esteem fears an unfavourable opinion from the group, and imagination very often sanctions criticism of this sort of its own accord. Hence the panic and failure.

A deep sense of fear and inferiority, for which there is no apparent historic or contemporary meaning, may be due to a repressed guilt complex — usually associated with sex. Various factors may be responsible for these deeply toned negative emotions which pervade the personality: Secret masturbation, the memory of some 'sin,' or a consciousness of some form of sexual inadequacy or perversion.

TREATMENT

Treatment of inferiority feeling will depend very greatly upon its conditions and nature.

1. If it finds expression in any form of anti-social feeling such as failure in social adjustment, or a flight from reality in drink, etc., it may be taken for granted that the sources of all such inferiority lie in wrong childhood training.

This is practically an axiom. A true and wise training in childhood never leads an individual to anti-social attitudes.

An analysis of childhood must be made, and the experiences which have formed the anti-social or inferiority feeling assessed. When through self-analysis or wise help this has been done, the whole personality must be re-educated in self-confidence, self-respect and self-reliance.

By persistent endeavour, patience and understanding, the old inferior ways of thinking and feeling can be eradicated and positive ways of thinking and feeling established. These we may describe as self-knowledge, self-reverence, and self-control.

2. In the fear which arises from inexperience it must be recognized that all such situations are alone satisfactorily solved by action. This action involves the possibility of temporary failure, but there is no other way of gaining experience, competence and courage.

To draw back from an experience because imagination pictures failure or embarrassment is to surrender the will to an aspect of individuality over which the enlightened and disciplined mind should be master.

Electricity uncontrolled devastates and destroys, but controlled and utilised it is productive of the highest good. No less is this true of the imagination.

In children, where experience is limited, imagination may predominate and influence conduct in certain situations, but the adult should recognize imagination for what it is and have it under control.

If, as the first occasion, we do not meet the new experience with complete success or make a satisfactory adjustment, the setback should be looked upon in the light of a necessary lesson in achievement and courage.

The airman who crashes, if he can do so at all, immediately goes up again. It has been found that if he does not do this a certain amount of self-confidence is lost. The memory of the failure sinks into the unconscious mind in the intervening period and establishes a fear complex.

If we crash on an occasion when speaking, singing, performing, learning, in responding to experience in any form, we should — with the airman — immediately 'go up again'. By this adventurous and courageous attitude, we keep our nerve, attain results, and make progress in our efforts toward any goal or ideal.

3. The individual dominated by a deep sense of personal inadequacy by his persistent negative feeling, declares that there is some aspect of his psychical life in a state of emotional disintegration. Freud would have it that a persistent sense of emotional inadequacy has its roots in some form of sex disharmony.

In the next chapter we shall deal with this condition more fully under the category of anxiety.

3.
Fear and Anxiety

AS we have already observed, anxiety is a form of neurotic fear, and neurotic fear may be defined as fear which has no substance or basis in external fact. We have shown the difference between normal and neurotic fear.

The fear that is normal preserves life and makes for progress. The railway signalman who has the safety of so many lives in his hands is afraid of making a mistake in his signals. His fear makes him careful and efficient. But his fear may also inspire him to invent a new mechanical safety appliance whereby the lives of thousands are given a greater security.

The surgeon who has to perform a delicate operation acquaints himself with every phase of the subject. If, by his knowledge and care, he becomes an outstanding surgeon fear for his own reputation and the life of his patient makes for progress and preservation. Normal fear has therefore a social and personal value and is healthy.

But if any of these people allowed fear to paralyze their initiative and capacity so that they gave up their positions, we should say immediately that they were neurotic, and we should look for the source of the trouble, not in the work which they declare is dangerous (yet is being and has to be done by multitudes every day), but in some inner disintegration of the individual's private psychical life.

Their neurotic fear is a 'displacement' of an inner emotional sense of inadequacy. Psychic emotional strain or tension (anxiety) is always due to repression.

CONDITIONS OF ANXIETY

Anxiety can be for convenience divided theoretically into three forms of expression: Anxiety hysteria, anxiety repression, and worry. These three forms cover to a greater or lesser degree the various conditions of anxiety.

In practice no such division is possible since anxiety is a condition of the psyche with various qualities and characteristics of expression according to the particular person and his problem.

Thus no uniform description can be laid down as a rigid exposition of what anxiety really is or how it works. We know the principles and its causes; the rest is a matter of individual expression.

The leading form of anxiety is anxiety hysteria. Freud, who was the pioneer in this branch of investigation, describes the anxiety attack thus.

There may be: (a) disorders of the heart, chiefly palpitation; (b) disorders of the breathing, attacks like asthma, and so on — Freud mentions that even these attacks are not always accompanied by recognizable anxiety; (c) attacks of excessive sweating, often at night; (d) attacks of trembling and shaking, which may easily be taken for hysteria; (e) sudden attacks of diarrhoea; (f) attacks of giddiness; (g) sudden fright on awakening from sleep, as if falling from a mountain; (h) muscular cramp.

Stekel, who worked on a considerable number of anxiety cases, gave the following symptoms in addition: (i) Sudden deep sighs, the result of breathlessness, often amounting to air-hunger; (j) the sudden on-coming of a feeling of weariness, that can amount to faintness; (k) vomiting and stomach ache, also painful flatulency, with the noisy passing of large quantities of wind; (l) the fingers suddenly become dead, or the whole hand or arm; (m) migraine which causes headache accompanied by nausea; (n) great restlessness, aimless running about.

It has been established that anxiety conditions are mainly due to some form of injurious sex life (of which there are so many), erotic excitement, rigid abstinence, frustration, etc. Other factors are a loveless marriage, disgust and repugnance to the partner or a repressed perversion.

Allied with anxiety hysteria is anxiety repression. Anxiety repression has many similarities with hysteria, both in causation and characteristics. It brings a general sense of discomfort, extreme irritability and kindred negative conditions.

We have for instance the case of a patient who was haunted by the fear that his business was going to pieces. Investigation showed that it was on a thoroughly sound basis. Deeper investigation showed that he was toying with the thought of leaving his wife and going off with an attractive young business acquaintance.

By the mental mechanism of 'displacement' he displaced this thought in his mind by associating it with his business breaking down. The real cause of his anxiety was the dreaded breakdown of his marriage.

Another such illustration is that of the young man 'who could not stand the country.' He lived at home with his parents, who in their outlook were rather religiously rigid and old-fashioned.

Investigation showed that his restlessness, lack of interest at home and failure to stand the country which was 'so slow,' was really a displaced desire to be in a big city, where away from parental restraints and control he could live a little 'faster.'

Symptoms of anxiety repression may also arise when the individual is afraid of a situation, event or experience. A woman who was shortly to undergo an operation lived in a continual state of nerves and tension. The least incident threw her into a panic. In everyday things nothing was just right, everything a little wrong.

Something unknown and fearsome was always going to happen.

She was really projecting her inner dread and uncertainty upon the environment.

Worry, which was our third category, is the most general expression of anxiety. In the main its causes may be traced to three sources: An unconscious fear of disaster, physical, social or economic; an unconscious repression of the libido or life urge; an unconscious sense of guilt.

APPREHENSION

We have just given an illustration of how the sense of dread can produce a persistent worrying about events and things which without this undertone of apprehension should cause no worry at all.

It is not too much to say that worry over health is one of the distinguishing features of civilization. By skilfully worded advertisements the great patent medicine combines have created a health neurosis which will guarantee dividends to their concerns during the tenure of their existence.

It would be an interesting diversion to endeavour to assess — if it were possible — whether there has been more pain and worry caused by these advertisements than has been alleviated by their declared powers of healing.

'Keeping up appearances' is another modern worry. For very many social life has become so self-conscious and delicate that any drop in the scale is attended by mental conditions not far removed from a neurosis. Instead of snapping their fingers at the fetish of public opinion by living their life sensibly at their own possible level, many people worry themselves in a childish immature attempt to maintain an almost impossible standard.

To the slave of public opinion the robust attitude of Nietzsche acts as a tonic: 'I am thus; I shall be thus, and the rest of you can go hang!'

St. John Ervine vividly described in one of his stories how uncontrolled worry could take all the savour out of life.

The existence of Mr. Timms, a clerk in a London office, revolved continually round the thought: Supposing that one day he should be unable to work, what would become of him? He would awaken at night crying out in fear because of some horrible dream in which he saw himself dismissed.

The same terror was his evil genius by day. As the years passed the despotism of this fear took heavy toll of the best possibilities of his life. Something inside him would urge him to the quest of adventure. 'Do something to show that you are alive,' it would say, and the fear of endangering his position by some time yielding to one of these moods added another to his many terrors.

He thought of marriage, and the thing inside him kept saying: 'Risk it, man, risk it!' But the thought of the possibility of getting sick and out of employment with a wife and perhaps a family to support, drove him back to the dreariness of his dingy bed-sitting-room.

Finally, the inevitable came: He lost his position, and his savings rapidly dwindled. Sickness overtook him, and the doctor's verdict was that he had only a short time to live.

The doctor was amazed at the calm which the announcement brought.

'Thank God,' said Mr. Timms to himself. 'I am safe now.' In three months he was dead.

For many unmarried people of both sexes, but particularly young unmarried females, repression of the instinctive desires leads to many forms of conflict and psychical distress, which are covered by the familiar word 'worry.'

The popular joke of the spinster who looked beneath the bed each night to see if there was a burglar expresses a psychological tragedy as well as a social comedy.

Even before Freud's day, such writers as Krafft-Ebing, Myström, Rolileder, Kisch and Leyden noticed that repression resulted in states of anxiety and nervousness.

GUILT COMPLEX

A secret sense of guilt is well known as the cause of worry and its kindred states of restlessness, involuntary fears, suspicion, etc. The man with a guilty conscience lives in a continual state of suspense and anxiety.

A sense of guilt may be either conscious or unconscious. It may arise from a criminal act in the present, of which the individual is only too aware. It is this immediate awareness that makes him afraid both of his own conscience and the law.

On the other hand, the guilt feeling may be nothing more than a dim unconscious feeling which has its source in some forbidden act of childhood which has established a guilt complex in the unconscious mind.

The guilt complex creates a sense of tension, conflict, disharmony and very often discomfiture in the presence of others. It is the preponderate cause of chronic cases of self-consciousness.

We have read of a farmer who, when driving slowly along the road that led to the town, was met by a neighbour, who hailed him and asked where he was going.

'I'm going to the village to get drunk,' replied Jim gloomily, 'and gosh, how I dread it!'

The world is full of people like Jim, who, driven against their best selves, endeavour to solve or resolve their inner problems and difficulties by an escape into alcohol.

The treatment of anxiety will follow upon the nature and character of the anxiety condition. Let us examine both sides of the question in its various forms.

1. The truth should be faced frankly and sensibly that the sex instinct is so strong and deeply rooted in Nature because it is essential to Nature. The preservation of the race is bound up

with its strength and expression.

When in man it moves through its successive stages of development naturally and normally, and at maturity reaches out for fulfilment by social sanction and love, it is the most beautiful and stimulating power in the world.

When, however, it becomes frustrated or perverted in development and expression it can destroy both psychical and physical well-being.

Where the love-life is natural and sincere there is usually no neurosis. Freud has laid this down as an axiom.

Where marriage is impossible — for whatever reason — an endeavour should be made to sublimate the instinctive desires by devotion to social welfare, religious work and intellectual occupations, or the pursuit of a creative hobby that engages all the interest of the individual.

In this way the over-plus of nervous energy which is the by-product of life on its animal side is sublimated, transformed and released.

CREATIVE OUTLET

For both physical and psychical health it is extremely important that the dynamic energies should be released in creative forms. If they are not they become pent up within the unconscious and stagnate or find an outlet in neurotic conditions.

Compare the Sea of Galilee with the Dead Sea. In the waters of Galilee fish abound, and its banks are fertile. The Dead Sea waters on the other hand are so salty that nothing can live in them, and its banks are barren.

The reason is that the Sea of Galilee not only gathers waters from tributaries, but also gives them release by outlets which keep the water fresh and wholesome. The Dead Sea gathers its waters from tributaries, but because it has no outlet beyond evaporation it is stagnant and over-salty.

This is a parable of the human personality. The very frequent remarks that life has no meaning, has lost all interest, is profoundly unreal, nothing is worthwhile, etc., which we sometimes hear, are a confession that the personality has become like the Dead Sea — it gathers powers from Nature and the environment, but does not give them back again in social usefulness and creativity.

Where, however, the source or secret of persistent anxiety cannot be traced — certain physical conditions sometimes are a predisposing cause — the patient should consult a competent medical psychotherapist.

The deepest motives, interests and desires of the soul must be laid bare and the human spirit cleansed from its accumulated emotional poisons. When by a purging of the spirit these poisons are removed, health of mind, soul and body are restored.

2. The sensible thing to do about health if it gives us concern is to get the advice of a doctor and follow it. If after we have been examined

and our fears dispelled we still continue to worry, it may be taken that our real worry lies deeper and has to do with our psychical rather than our physical health.

It is poor advice merely to tell anyone to stop worrying. No one worries by will; no one wishes to worry. No one wishes to live under a continual strain and tension, fretting and irritable over trifling incidents and situations.

People only live so because deep in their soul there lies buried a fear thought, a complex of which they are consciously unaware. It may be, of course, that they are aware of the inner disturbance, but they are afraid to face it.

It would have been futile, for instance, to have told Lady Macbeth to stop worrying. In the soul of Lady Macbeth there was a conflict between her conscience and the memory of her participation in a dastardly crime. Until that conflict was settled one way or other there could be no peace for her.

In like manner, where there is a hidden conflict in the unconscious mind, a conflict between the moral ego (conscience) and instinctive desire, or between ethical conduct and a wish, or between what we know we should do and what we are afraid to do, there will be worry.

Worry has its roots in a personal problem either conscious or unconscious. The primary need to remove worry is the settlement or eradication of the unconscious problem, fear or emotional distress.

4.
Fear and the Phobias

IT has been estimated that one out of every ten persons is beset by a special fear of one kind or another. It is these peculiar private fears that are called phobias. The original word in Greek is *phobos*, meaning fear. Modern psychological usage, however, applies the word more particularly to fears which are private, peculiar and irrational.

The distinction between normal fear, anxiety and the phobias may be briefly stated thus. A normal fear is aroused when some external object or situation threatens the existence of the individual. The emotion of fear on these occasions is perfectly natural, as by its awareness preparation is made for either flight or defence; thereby the individual preserves his own life and that of the race.

Anxiety, and its various expressions, is aroused when there is no external object or situation to justify any kind of negative feeling or disturbance. It is rather a persistent subjective sense of emotional discomfort and apprehension. Quite frequently bodily symptoms are associated with the feeling, and the victim believes that his anxiety distress is due to some physical defect, disease or weakness. This is, of course, the reverse of the truth.

A phobia, on the other hand, has its originating and stimulating cause in the environment, but the object or person which is the cause of the fear to the neurotic is usually treated by the normal person as quite harmless or of no consequence.

We have, for instance, the well-known fact that some people are driven almost frantic by mice and cats. Ordinary people look upon mice and cats as of no consequence, at least of not so much consequence as to drive them into a panic. To the sufferer from a phobia, however, they constitute a menace.

Phobias are due to emotionally toned repressed ideas, 'complexes' to which the individual has not become adjusted. Whatever we leave unexpressed or unsolved in the course of life we leave in the unconscious. If we had expressed the thought, or idea, it would have passed out into society in personal fulfilment. If we are afraid of the thought or idea and repress it into the unconscious, the emotion associated with the idea lives on in the hinterland of the mind.

Because thought, in one aspect of it, has its inspiration and genesis in feeling, the emotions associated with the repressed ideas find expression in thoughts and actions that are irrational or abnormal.

A phobia is, therefore, the feeling associated with a repressed hurtful idea or memory which is stimulated in the unconscious by objects or situations which in some private way symbolize and energize the original repressed fear.

This will be made clear in an illustration of claustrophobia.

CLASSIFICATION OF PHOBIAS

Phobias may be classified into two categories: Obsessions and compulsions. Under obsessions we have phobias of situations, objects, ideas and of the body.

Phobias of situation are legion. Two will be sufficient to make the condition clear: Claustrophobia, the fear of closed spaces, i.e. tunnels, rooms, theatres, etc.; and agoraphobia, the fear of open spaces, i.e. streets, land, sea, etc.

An interesting example of claustrophobia is that by Rivers, quoted by McDougall, as it demonstrates very clearly the influence of repressed emotionally toned memories and ideas, running back into childhood. We shall quote the illustration in full.

A medical man of thirty-one years had suffered since childhood some discomfort, sometimes amounting to very distinct fear, whenever confined in a narrow space. He regarded this as normal. He also suffered at times from general nervousness and stammering; and, in order to obtain relief from these, he had at one time undergone treatment.

During the war he served at the front, and there he had to spend much of his time in dug-outs. He found this very trying, and often spent the night wandering in the trench, rather than remain in his dug-out.

He now realized for the first time that his fear of closed spaces was a morbid symptom. His condition became so bad that he was sent to hospital, with insomnia, stammering, battle-dreams, depression, headache, etc.

Rivers instructed him to record his dreams, and also to try to recover early memories in connection with his dreams. After a short course of such efforts he remembered, in thinking over a dream, a childish experience (of his fourth year) which he had never before recollected in the course of his endeavours to throw light on his condition.

The incident which he remembered was a visit to an old rag-and-bone merchant, who lived near the house which his parents then occupied. This old man was in the habit of giving boys a halfpenny when they took to him something of value.

The child had found something and had taken it along to the house of the old man. He had been admitted through a dark narrow passage. At the end of the passage was a brown spaniel. Having received his reward, the child came out alone to find the door of exit to the street shut. He was too small to open the door, and the dog at the other end of the passage began to growl. The child was terrified.

His state of terror came back to him vividly as the incident returned to his mind after the many years of oblivion. The influence which the incident made on his mind is shown by his recollection that ever afterwards he was afraid to pass the house of the old man.

A few days later, as he lay thinking over another dream, he found himself repeating the name 'Mr. Cann'; and then he remembered that this was the name of the old rag-and-bone merchant.

This forgotten experience of childhood was the source of his phobia — the fear of closed spaces. From the moment of the recovery of this memory, which as we have seen was deeply toned with feeling, the phobia was greatly weakened.

The point to note in this illustration is that the consciousness of being in a narrow space — the dug-out — stimulated feelings associated with a childhood experience which the conscious mind had to all intents and purposes completely forgotten. When, however, the conscious mind saw the connection between and the meaning of the childhood experience with present feeling, the phobia lost its power.

All previous effort of one form and another was useless and ineffective. Only when the conscious mind recognized the origin of the fear was the complex released and mastery gained over the mind.

Similarly in all cases of this kind no amount of mental rules, however good or however faithfully followed, are of any use until the buried emotional complex, which is the cause of the trouble, is released.

AGORAPHOBIA

Stekel recorded a striking case of agoraphobia (the fear of open spaces):

A tall, well-built man, twenty years of age suffered from an acute fear of open spaces. This man stopped at every open place, began to shake, and no power on earth could induce him to cross alone, although he could manage it accompanied by another person.

Investigation revealed that his parents were very poor, that he supported and was very fond of them. It also revealed that he had played with the idea of stealing some money and going off.

His anxiety arose from a repressed desire to abscond to America with a large sum of money. The open space suggested to his mind the flight to America. His shaking and fear was stimulated by association in his unconscious mind with the consequences of his act.

Two facts lie at the basis of both compulsions and obsessions. Both have their meaning in repressed emotionally toned ideas, memories, thoughts, etc., of which individuals are afraid. They are afraid of these repressed ideas because in some way they are repugnant to the moral ego.

McDougall is of the opinion that every phobia has also a guilt association. Freud declared: 'Obsessions are always reproaches re-emerging in a transmuted form under repression'. Stekel was more emphatic and insisted: 'The consciousness of guilt is the chief cause of all neuroses and psychoses.'

Phobias of objects are as legion as those of situations. The objects feared cover everything conceivable, most of which are harmless in themselves. In fact some people have an obsession technically called panta-phobia, the fear of anything and everything!

Obsessive fear of objects is shared by people in all walks of life. John Bunyan, one-time tinker of Bedford, tells in his book, *Grace Abounding*, how in his unconverted days he took great pleasure in ringing the bells of the parish church at Elstow.

Ultimately he developed a conscience in the matter, and came to feel it was wrong. He contracted a phobia characterized by a terrible fear of seeing or hearing bells.

At the other end of the social ladder King James had a neurotic fear of swords. When knighting with the naked sword his hand shook, and he felt he might stick the sword into the kneeling figure. So afraid was he, he closed his eyes during the ceremony and had his shaking hand guided in the ceremonial act.

It is on record that Caesar's whole body

trembled when it began to thunder. He fled to the deepest cellar in his palace and covered his head with thick furs, so that he might not hear the thunder-claps.

Erasmus was horrified if he saw a fish, and Pascal was afraid of a thousand and one things. Frederick the Great had an aversion for all new clothing or new uniforms.

Newton was sick on encountering water. Mozart ran away at the sound of a trumpet or hunting-horn. Schopenhauer trembled at the sight of a razor. Carlyle never dared to set foot in a shop; although a keen critic of heroes and heroic deeds, he was afraid of an ordinary shop-keeper.

Edgar Allan Poe, Schumann and Chopin were all afraid of the dark. Maupassant had a fear and horror of doors.

PHOBIAS OF IDEAS

Phobias of ideas are quite common and psychologically very interesting. Many people are haunted with the fear that they are going insane.

Such phobias are the displaced expression of guilty feelings, thoughts and desires, which surge within the unconscious mind but become transformed by the censorship of the conscious mind.

This mental mechanism follows the well-known mental law that a person who has no hesitation in robbing another man is suspicious that every other man is bent on the same unethical conduct. His own attitude to life colours his interpretation of another man's attitude.

Phobias of the body are very general. Though the patient has been given the assurance by his doctor that there is nothing organically wrong with him, he still persists in believing that he has a cancerous growth, heart trouble, stomach trouble, etc.

In very many cases the unconscious mind creates the symptoms in response to the fear, so that these 'conversion' pains are looked upon as infallible indications that something very serious is the matter.

COMPULSIONS

Akin to and arising from obsessive fears we have compulsions. The difference between an obsession and a compulsion is that an obsession is *felt* while a compulsion is *acted out*.

In an obsession the fear is private and inward, in a compulsion the fear (or desire that is taboo) is given a symbolical form in an act. In an obsession a cat or a knife may be the symbol that arouses the feeling of fear; in the compulsion the individual creates his own symbol.

Compulsions like obsessions cover every conceivable subject, object or situation. The travelling compulsive must sit in a certain seat in a certain way in a certain carriage. The fadistic compulsive must eat certain food in a certain way at a certain time. The erotic compulsive must love in a certain way according to an established ritual.

The repetitive compulsive performs a particular act over and over again: Must touch every lamp-post on his way home, count his money over and over again, etc. Any failure in the established order his unconscious mind has built up throws him into a panic.

The sadistic compulsive must hurt someone in a certain way; and the methodical compulsive must do her housework or his office work by a routine from which there can be no deviation.

As we have seen, both obsessions and compulsions are substitutes for something desired, or imagined, that does not harmonize with the personality ego. The desired thing or hurtful thought has been repressed into the unconscious mind, but because it is so strongly desired or has not been adequately dealt with by the conscious mind, it keeps fermenting in the depth of the psyche and endeavours to find fulfilment and expression in these phobias.

The fear associated with every phobia is really the condemnation by the super-ego or conscience of the ego for harbouring such unethical wishes. The fear may also be a fear of detection.

SEEKING OUT THE CAUSE

The prime necessity in any treatment of these conditions is to discover the root of the trouble. This is usually difficult for the mind untrained in psychological meanings with no personal powers of introspection or insight.

The trained psychologist, however, can read at a glance the significance of most of the actions which lie behind the compulsive ritual. He translates the symbolic act into psychological meanings, for he can see that the compulsive act is really a little play with personal motives and intentions lying behind the dramatization.

Through a utilization of psychological technique such as free-association, dream analysis and hypnotism, he can also lay bare the meanings of the obsession.

We advise anyone who is the victim of either a disturbing obsession or compulsion to put himself in the hands of a skilled psychotherapist. All the advice in the world about the training of the will and imagination will be completely ineffective until the buried complex, which is the root cause of the trouble, is either dispelled or released.

When this is accomplished the mind of its own accord responds normally and adequately to the flow of growing life; just as a stream responds normally and adequately when the obstructions that impede its progress are removed.

Yet, while an obsession or compulsion may be due to a buried complex perhaps running back into childhood, it is also true that it may be due to an unethical attitude to life which the individual does not want to face or eradicate.

The victim, or more truly the patient, is harbouring a secret vice, desire, craving which he tolerates because he is either its slave or will not master it. He, as religion says, 'hugs his sin.'

The leading psychological thinkers are agreed on this fact as we have shown. The remedy in all these cases is in the hands of the individual.

5.
Fear and Fortitude

IN the previous chapters we have dealt mainly with what may be termed morbid fears, that is to say with fears which are abnormal and personally disturbing. But while it is estimated that one person in every ten suffers from an abnormal fear of some kind, it is also true that there are very many haunted by fears which cannot be placed in the category of the abnormal.

The fear with which they are afflicted is rather a persistent dread and feeling that something is going to happen for which they will be unprepared. : Frequently these dreads in women may be nothing other than displaced desires; and not infrequently in all individuals the sign of a guilty conscience. But these explanations do not account for the extent and universality of these twilight anxieties.

Most of these feelings of insecurity and inferiority arise from the stress and strain of the modern world and the exacting nature of modern civilization.

Existence for most people has become very intense and complicated. Every aspect of it, to the extremely socially self-conscious, threatens the human ego.

Socially the modern man must maintain his prestige. He fears acutely any loss of an exagerated self-importance which he has built around his usually commonplace ego.

Physically he is aware of the insecurity of his tenure upon the earth. Economically he lives with the dread that all he has built up will fall to pieces at his feet through no fault of his own.

Consequently the modern man lives under the strain of an intangible fear that every moment is potent with danger — that the unknown holds a threat against him. The restlessness and fever of the age declare that man has yet to win his soul and come to terms with his environment.

Here is how one man met this situation. Being of a realistic turn of mind and wishing to look at things from an analytical point of view, he decided to put his fears on paper and examine them critically and coolly. At the top of the list he put all those dire disasters about which he had worried himself well-nigh sick, but which, as later events proved, never happened. These fears he estimated to comprise at least 40 per cent of the list.

Next in order he set down the decisions he had made in the past, decisions, of course, about which he could now do nothing; fears lest he had done the wrong thing, or taken the wrong path. These he calculated were 30 per cent. of his trouble.

As the third item he counted in all his forebodings about possible sickness, probable bankruptcy and nervous breakdown, fear that he might not be equal to his job and fail to 'deliver the goods,' none of which had materialized to date. These added up to 12 per cent.

Nor did he forget his worries about his children and friends — worries, as he discovered, due to the fact that he did not give people credit for having an ordinary amount of common sense. These he estimated to be 10 per cent.

At the bottom of the list he put down the worries that had a real foundation, and with which he would have to deal, and he found, to his surprise, that *they were only 8 per cent of the total.*

When he eliminated the 92 per cent imaginary fears, he discovered that he could quite adequately handle the 8 per cent real fears. He found that in life, as in golf, most people are beaten by 'bogey.'

A TRUE RELIGION

Psychologists now recognize the helpful power of a true religion in giving men and women fortitude and faith to meet the challenge of life.

There is a growing conviction that much of the neurotic condition and outlook of this age is due to the fact that in losing faith in God men and women have lost faith in themselves and their neighbours.

That is to say they have no background of confidence outside themselves, so that when they are confronted with a crisis or emergency which proves too big for them, they are left with nothing but the various forms of despair as an escape, namely, drink, drugs, suicide and insanity.

One of the greatest of modern psychologists, Jung, whose words in this connection must be considered said: 'Among all my patients in the second half of life — that is to say, over thirty-five — there has not been one whose problem in the last resort was not that of finding a religious outlook on life.

'It is safe to say that every one of them fell ill because he had lost that which the living religions of every age have given to their followers, and none of them has been really healed who did not regain his religious outlook.'

The noted London psychologist, Dr. Hadfield, came to the same conclusion after years of experience in psychotherapeutic healing.

He said: 'Speaking as a student of psychotherapy, who, as such, has no concern with theology, I am convinced that the Christian religion is one of the most valuable and potent influences that we possess for producing that harmony and peace of mind and that confidence of soul which is needed to bring health and power to a large number of nervous persons.

'I have attempted to cure nervous patients with suggestions of quietness and confidence, but without success until I have linked those suggestions on to that faith in the power of God which is the substance of the Christian confidence and hope. Then the patient has become strong.'

To combat the fear that dominates the human spirit there is needed a faith. If an individual fears life what power is there in the world — no matter what its name may be — that will transform this fear into faith, fortitude and courage?

Psychology only shows what is wrong; the individual stands confessed that he cannot help himself, otherwise he would not be in his now desperate condition. As Dr. Adler has demonstrated, the feeling of insecurity and inferiority is universal and native to the human being, so that by his very constitution he is in need of a reserve and power not his own to help him to manage life.

True religion has always given to men and women a sense of mastery. It has transformed the sense of insecurity and fear into one of confidence and faith. The man of faith feels supported by all the resources of the universe and through these is saved from panic and despair.

Do's and Don'ts
for the Fearful

1. DON'T think that fear is something external that is actively destructive.
   DO recognize that fear only exists in your mind and is an expression of your dynamic attitude to reality.
2. DON'T think that you can escape without effort the unconsciously acquired fears of childhood.
   DO recognize that your present fear of the dark and the unknown is but the working out from the unconscious mind of those harmful suggestions and experiences.
3. DON'T think that because you have failed once or twice through lack of confidence due to wrong training in childhood that you must always fail.
   DO recognize that as a mature person you can recondition your mental outlook and rebuild a courageous attitude that conquers fear and difficulties.
4. DON'T think that nervous anxiety has some-

thing to do with material nerves and can be cured by medicine.

DO recognize that this condition indicates the presence of a situation of which you are afraid, or indicates a wrong way of living which must be put right.

5. DON'T think that an obsession or compulsion is a weakness inherited from your parents.

DO recognize that both are the emotional expression of unconscious guilt reproaches or unconscious unethical wishes.

6. DON'T think that you must always be the victim of fear and that you can look for no help beyond yourself.

DO recognize that there is a power beyond your own that is effective in life and that millions through faith in that power have found peace of soul and brought poise to their personalities.

Other recommended books...

CONQUERING NERVOUS TENSION

Wilfrid Northfield. Millions of people fail to get the best out of life because of 'nerves'. They wake up tired ; jump at the slightest sound ; cannot concentrate ; and lie awake at night, worrying. Nerves are the connecting link between brain and body, like an intricate system of telegraph wires. There are cases of disease in the nerves, but these are comparatively rare. When your nerves are wrong it does not mean that these physical 'telegraphs' are diseased, but that the messages running along them are 'tied up in knots'. The purpose of this book is to 'unravel' these knots. *Contents include:* Secret disease of today ; Learn to relax ; Excessive nervous tension ; Mental control ; Energy reserves ; Mind-wandering ; Nature's energy-rhythm.

CONQUER SHYNESS

C. H. Teear, B.A. Shy people are frightened people because they are always unsure of themselves ; they are unable to go out and enjoy a proper social life. They feel themselves to be separated from others by a psychological barrier which is wholly self-erected and which usually has its origin in some unfortunate childhood experience. This book presents a plan of campaign to help those afflicted with shyness to understand themselves and take practical steps for over-coming their handicap. *Contents include:* The urge for friendship ; Analyzing your childhood ; The centre of attention ; Live longer and happier ; Trembling and blushing ; Magnetic personalities ; The opposite sex ; Possessive friendship ; Building up friendships ; Coping with unkindness ; Entering and leaving a room ; Listen to others.

OVERCOMING STAMMERING

R. MacDonald Ladell, M.D., Ch.B. Stammering is a neurosis, not due to organic defect but to emotional reaction, and has its roots in childhood. It results from an internal conflict between conscious and subconscious urges dating back to the sufferer's formative years, when he—perhaps through parental suppression—was not allowed to assert his personality and became shy, developing a basic urge to keep silent. The resulting feeling of inferiority was imprinted on the unconscious mind and the stammer adopted as a childish defence mechanism. Curing the stammer requires the employment of practical psychological techniques which are clearly explained here, not only for adolescent and adult stammerers, but also for the guidance of teachers, parents or guardians of a stammering child.

CONFIDENT SPEAKING

Margaret Perkins. Speech, to be readily understood anywhere in the British Isles, ought to conform as nearly as possible to what is known as standard English. We must retain our individuality, but when the occasion demands we should be able to speak fluently, without undue accent. By improving our voices and speech we find a more fitting outlet for our personalities. Then attention can be focused on the content and manner of speech, but—as with learning to play a muscial instrument—certain techniques need to be acquired before a melodious tune can be produced. *This book explains:* Consonants ; Vowels ; Pronunciation and emphasis ; Modulation ; Phrasing and pause ; Correct breathing ; Projecting your image ; Posture. Includes some hints on public speaking.

MAKING FRIENDS EASILY

C. H. Teear, B.A. Loneliness can be experienced in a crowded urban complex! Author reveals psychological 'blocks' which stop us making friends, gives practical measures for developing a positive personality, gaining new interests, banishing selfconsciousness. Nearly all the barriers existing between ourselves and neighbours are of our own making. This book explains how to demolish them once and for all! *Contents include:* Good friends are loyal; The face of friendship; Anti-social behaviour; When the mind turns inwards; Spirit of comradeship; This is a gentleman; Be a good listener; The value of small talk; Don't be a butterfly; Meeting new people; Admit your own faults; The old and the sick; Opportunities through the local church; Keep your sense of proportion.

THE POWER OF AUTO-SUGGESTION

Peter Fletcher. Auto-suggestion is a powerful tool for directing or changing human behaviour. If employed in the manner recommended by Peter Fletcher it can increase mental efficiency and bodily health; change old, bad habits for new, good ones; improve self-confidence; help us to become masters of our moods. This is because auto-suggestions call up all the energy of our imagination and so arouse our strongest feelings, providing we are able to imagine that what we suggest to ourselves will come true. For imagination is the motive force behind auto-suggestion, producing the psychological maxim: 'where the will and the imagination are in conflict, imagination always wins.' This provides a clue to the effective use of suggestion.

HOW TO RELAX

Wilfrid Northfield. How to acquire the benefits of complete relaxation. Author reveals how to regain lost self-control, become less impatient, enjoy tranquility, meet life with optimism and increase energy for work and play. Serenity, poise and increased efficiency can be ours through relaxation. This book contains a message that none of us can afford to ignore. The demands of modern living, particularly in towns and cities, are such that almost everyone suffers from some sort of tension. It is an occupational hazard. *Contents include:* Rhythmical breathing; Let yourself go; Importance of leisure; Sense of purpose; Anyone can relax; Thought control; The benefit of laughter; Banish anxious thoughts; 'Exciting' colours; Waste of nervous energy; The 'monotonous' job; Message to housewives.

THE POWER OF CREATIVE IMAGINATION

DYNAMIC SECRET OF SUCCESS

Leslie O. Korth, D.O. An exciting blueprint for achieving success and mental stability by substituting creative imagination for 'will-power'. The author explains how to achieve ambitions and eradicate bad habits (including drug addiction) by putting into practice the famous law of reversed effort formulated by the Frenchman Coué, who taught that whenever the imagination is in conflict with the will, the imagination always wins the day. *Contents include:* What is free will?; The 'ideal' as stimulus of will; Self comes first; Gestures—gateway to the soul; 'Freudian slips' betray real nature of innermost thoughts; Extraversion and introversion; Parassociations, taxisms and engrams; Conditioning determines destiny; Training the imagination.